MADBiz Asia Solutions
Delivering the *Difference* in
Your Business Results

A result-focused business improvement and
team development consulting firm

www.madbiz.org

MAD
in
Action

D. Lauren

WestBow
PRESS
A DIVISION OF THOMAS NELSON

ISBN: 978-1-4497-5399-3 (e)
ISBN: 978-1-4497-5400-6 (sc)

Library of Congress Control Number: 2012909331

WestBow Press books may be ordered through booksellers or by contacting:

WestBow Press
A Division of Thomas Nelson
1663 Liberty Drive
Bloomington, IN 47403
www.westbowpress.com
1-(866) 928-1240

Printed in the United States of America

WestBow Press rev. date: 05/29/2012

MAKING
A
DIFFERENCE
In your
BUSINESS

My Appreciation to..

My husband, Alvin, and daughter, Cailyn Michelle, who are a continuing source of inspiration for everything I do in life.

Thank you for being MAD in my life!

I dedicate this book
to
my dearest father, who has gone
to be with the Lord,
and to my wonderful mom ,
who always believes in and
encourages my dreams.
Dad, Mom,
thank you so much for everything.
I love you!

CONTENTS

From the **'MAD'** author ~10
What is **MADBiz** ~14

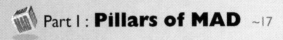

MAD keys to Building a Winning Team In Winning Customers

Welcome to
MAD CULTURE!

The Culture that
MAKES A DIFFERENCE.

First and foremost, I want to thank you for reading this book, **MADBiz : MAD in Action.**

This book is a continuation of my first book, **MADBiz : The MAD Culture**, which describes principles to effect change in organizational culture and how transformation in the work place can produce high performance and standards that ultimately result in delighting the customers. It outlines some innovative practices through several real-life management stories and case studies.

Before we understand what this second book, **MAD in Action**, is all about, we need to understand the term "organizational culture."

What is Organizational Culture?

An organization is made up of people. They are the ones who shape and deliver the organization's business performance. Their attitudes, behaviors, and their approach to work form the characteristics of the organization. In addition, a certain pattern or management structure or leadership style or traditions/legacies shape the behaviors and perceptions of the people in the organization. Over time, this forms the culture of the organization. Culture is also founded upon shared values, beliefs, assumptions, and expectations, which influence and affect the people's way of work and interaction with one another. Culture influences the way things are being done in an organization. "It's the way we do things here in order to get things done!"

Hence, before embarking on any business plan or strategy to grow or revive a business, it is essential to put into place the right mindset and heart set of the people in the organization. Having right thinking and doing will transform the climate of the organization and drive the people to perform above par.

Creating the **MAD CULTURE**

Changing a culture is tough enough—it is in the blood of the people, but creating a new culture is likened to performing blood transfusion many times over! The vision and strategies to transform the organization must be in the organization's DNA. A concerted effort and initiatives must be taken to incorporate the principles of **MADBiz** into every business and people's development plan. To successfully drive the **MAD Culture,** all levels of an organization's hierarchy should be engaged, intellectually and emotionally.

An organization that embraces a **MAD Culture** will surely produce a positive work climate that encourages and inspires its people to excellence.

What **MAD in ACTION** is all about

This book shares with you on **why** we must think and execute differently and **how** you can do it to generate the desired results. It gives some practical examples of making a difference in workplace and marketplace through personal experiences.

MAD in Action is a pictorial book containing more than one hundred illustrations and graphics for easy understanding and grasp of **MAD** principles and concepts; and for quick, simple recalls.

Are You **MAD?**

In the last chapter of this book, I have outlined some best practices on **"Building a WINNING TEAM in WINNING CUSTOMERS."** These are derived from my thirty years of work experience across the different major industries, as well as my encounters with different leadership in both national and global organizations. Just as I have greatly benefitted from this experience, I believe you will too.

As you read this book, let your mind be challenged by these questions:

- What type of culture is my organization?
- What type of culture am I developing in my workplace?
- Am I playing an active role to influence or change the culture of my organization?

Do I have a **MAD** mind, a **MAD** attitude, and a **MAD** spirit?
➡ Have I been **MAD** in my work?
➡ Am I **MAD** with my customers?
➡ How can I be more **MAD?**

It is my sincere wish that you will grab hold of the principles of **MADBiz** to create a **MAD** culture in your workplace and marketplace and for the personal enrichment of yourself. You have to be **MAD** in order to create the **MAD** Culture.

And yes! Don't forget to join the "The **MAD** Club." Visit our website for more information at www.madbiz.org.

Let's start our **MAD** journey!
D. Lauren

What is MADBiz?

MADBiz is not just a business approach.
Think of **MADBiz** as a way of life that you can embrace for
your own personal development as well as in your business.

MADBiz—an acronym for **"Making a Difference in your Business"** focuses on transforming people's behavior to create a healthy and positive organizational culture to deliver the desired results. It is based on the recognition that good culture is integral to the dynamic growth of an organization and is instrumental in building organizational effectiveness and efficiency.

MADBiz believes in creating a healthy climate, an exciting and fun workplace and making a difference in the marketplace as a result of changed thinking and doing. Albert Einstein said, "The significant problems we face cannot be solved at the same level of thinking we were at when we created them." Similarly, you cannot desire a change of results without changing the way you think and do things.
Think differently + act differently = generate different results.

MADBiz has adopted the signature line **"Top of the Mind and Core of the Heart"** to capture its strategy to consistently exceed not only the expectations of customers through the quality of your product or service but also in meeting their desires via your point of differentiation. The objective is to become the preferred solutions provider to your customers as well as their consumers.

While goals and strategies are easy to formulate, success hinges on effective implementation or execution. Many failures have their roots in poor execution.

MADBiz focuses on dynamic and creative executions. Intensity of focus, "see what is and not what seems to be," and consistency of purpose shape the desired results. Test it and see how it can transform your workplace and marketplace.

"When we remember
we are all mad,
the mysteries disappear
and life stands explained."

(Mark Twain)

Part I

PILLARS OF **MAD**

Build a **MAD** Culture through three pillars that form **MAD**

➤ **M**ind **M**odification
➤ **A**ttitude **A**lteration
➤ **D**esire **D**istinction

Then see the results they will have on your team members and your customers.

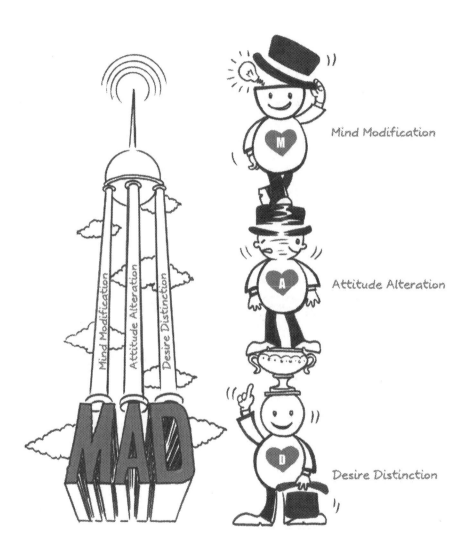

Mind Modification

Attitude Alteration

Desire Distinction

18

MIND MODIFICATION

- **Renewed Mind**
- **Creative Thinking**
- **Open Thinking**
- **Alternate Thinking**
- **Resourceful Mind**

MIND MODIFICATION

Ever feel like you have a mental block?
That you have to literally squeeze ideas from your mind?
Then it's time to renew your mind, which is the first stage of mind modification. Step in, throw away, and leave behind all the unnecessary baggage that has been weighing down the free flow of ideas.
You will walk out a completely different person.
One who feels refreshed, with a clearer vision and a wider perspective.
It's really all in the mind!

20

MIND MODIFICATION

Renewed Mind

Renewed Mind	Clear Mind	Clear Vision

In Depth Understanding

+

Sharp Discernment	Innovative Ideas & Solutions

+

Wider Perspective & Insights	Effective Decision Making

+

Right Thinking	Right Execution

High Growth Results

Mind renewal clears your mind. It leaves room for you to develop a clearer vision, better understanding, and adopt a wider perspective.
It paves the way for creative ideas, innovative solutions, and more effective decision-making.

MAD in Action

MIND MODIFICATION

A renewed mind is a renovated mind.
It does not look the same as before the renewal.
Like a renovated house, it has a new environment,
a new feel, and a new look.
It operates and conducts itself in a different
manner—more positively, more insightfully—and is
able to produce more inspired thoughts.

MIND MODIFICATION

Mediocre thinking and ordinary execution

produce mediocre results

Creative thinking and excellent execution

produce extraordinary results

You take out what you put in.
If your thinking is mediocre and your execution ordinary,
be prepared to accept mediocre results.
It is only through creativity that is carefully and purposefully
executed that we can expect something extraordinary.

Creative people do not see the world only in black and white. Their world is colourful; their skies always have a rainbow.
Sometimes they go against the flow of the majority, but that does not indicate that they are on the wrong track!

MAD in Action

MIND MODIFICATION

Creative Thinking

Values ideas and challenges status quo

Stretches capacity and ability of thoughts

Not afraid of embracing new, ambiguous ideas

Expands your world and charts new territories

Produces hope for the better

Ability to connect two unrelated or not similar ideas into one great feasible solution

Creates! They have creative power!

In creative thinking, be prepared to challenge the status quo and push the boundaries of conventional thinking. Be bold and unafraid of ideas that buck the trend. Expand your horizons to go where you have never gone before. Connect the dots, even when they seem unrelated. You may just hit on a brilliant idea!
Tap your creative powers!

24

MAD in Action

MIND MODIFICATION

Who would have thought just ten years ago that it could be possible to call, listen to music, access the Internet, retrieve your work and view videos all in a single mobile phone?
This has changed the way we work, play, and live.
That is the power of creative thinking, which helps us to break barriers, stretch the limits of possibilities, and challenge accepted norms.
So tap into the recesses of your mind and unlock your imagination.
Let your juices flow!

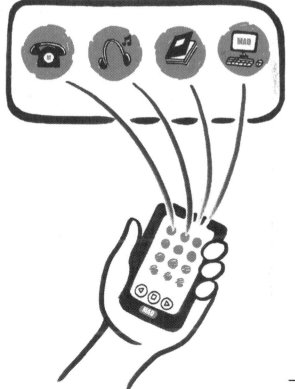

25

MAD in Action

MIND MODIFICATION

Like a sealed box, a closed mind is one where nothing goes in and nothing comes out! You become stuck in the same frame of mind, regurgitating the same ideas over and over again. Cut away the seals to open up your mind to allow fresh input for a refreshed output! You will see things in a whole new, different light!

MAD in Action

MIND MODIFICATION

Open thinking
=> doesn't restrict mind
=> looks expansively
=> explores all possibilities
=> scan against objectives

Open thinking explores a whole new world of thinking. It looks expansively and unrestrainedly at new horizons. It does not restrict its thinking. It seeks and finds new ways or solutions to problems.

Open thinking helps you to break out and explore every possibility, to see what works and what doesn't. It enables you to take new roads to meeting your objectives.

An open mind is receptive to receiving advice from others, to learn the right and the best options to pursue to achieve objectives.

MAD in Action

MIND MODIFICATION

A closed mind is like a prison. You're not free to move around and explore. Closed thinking leads to a fear and rejection of the unknown, untried and untested. It blocks the free flow of thinking and stifles creativity and originality.

Closed Thinking

➜ restricts the mind ➜ produces mental block ➜ rejects or refuses to receive new ideas, ways, or solutions to an issue ➜ produces below par results

Open thinking

➜ fertile soil to sow seeds for ideas, solutions, new ways of doing things ➜ good cultivation (in-depth understanding and insights, leverage and maximize resources, strategic executions) ➜ reap fruits (desired results) ➜ good harvest (high growth and contribution)

Open thinking sows the seeds for the cultivation of new ideas, solutions, and approaches to doing things. You gain a better understanding of how to leverage and maximize your resources and carry out strategic executions to reap the desired fruits of your labor and enjoy a harvest of high growth.

28

Mind Modification

Alternative Thinking

Most times, alternative thinking needs added focus, accuracy, and skill and requires boldness and strength to dare take on a new way of thinking and doing.

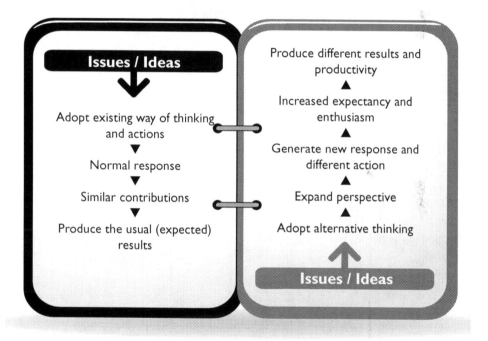

Issues / Ideas
↓
Adopt existing way of thinking and actions
▼
Normal response
▼
Similar contributions
▼
Produce the usual (expected) results

Produce different results and productivity
▲
Increased expectancy and enthusiasm
▲
Generate new response and different action
▲
Expand perspective
▲
Adopt alternative thinking
↑
Issues / Ideas

Don't stay with a one-track mind!

Sticking with the same way of doing things will only produce the usual results. Tweak it a bit with alternative thoughts and ideas to generate different results.

29

Mind Modification

As the saying goes, there is more than one way to skin a cat.

Likewise, there is more than one route or one mode of transportation to reach the same destination. Familiarity leads to complacency, preventing us from doing things better and achieving goals faster.

With alternative thinking, we are encouraged to step out of our comfort zone. By taking a different path, we open the door to improvement and new opportunities. In today's fast-moving world of business, those who choose to try new methods can surge ahead, while those who are afraid to will be left in the wake.

MAD in Action

MIND MODIFICATION

Often, we neglect to identify the gaps between what we have now and what is truly needed to achieve our objectives. We must gather and align our resources with our objectives or the purpose of the project.

Our work can be more effective and can reap higher productivity if we leverage on others' resources and skills. To achieve more, we cannot always depend on our own expertise and what we have. We need to be humble to tap onto others' skills, resources, expertise, and support to acquire the extra miles of success.

Always remain humble and trustworthy with everyone. The day may come when you need to knock on their door for support. People are bridges to achieving your calling (or dreams). So, do not burn bridges!

31

MIND MODIFICATION

A resourceful mind seeks to use everything
at its disposal to achieve its objectives. Look
at what you have and what you lack.
Use your existing resources before looking
elsewhere to fill the gap.

You may already have what it takes to achieve
your goals. You just may not be aware of it.
Before you fish outside for what you need, try
taking stock of your existing resources.

They may have been underutilized, misplaced,
or misused. Leverage on your resources by
maximizing their use. In this way, you can
expand your catch before extending your
reach.

MIND MODIFICATION

Resourceful Mind

A resourceful mind can extend out to every direction in the search for solutions. It looks at all options on the table, plugging the gaps as it identifies what needs to be done, how these things can be done, and what is needed to get it done!

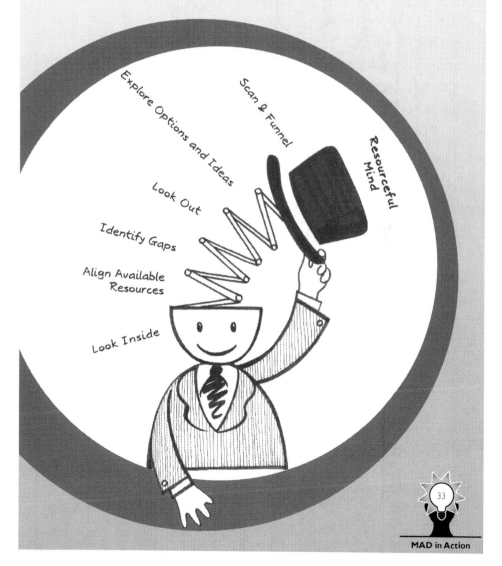

Explore Options and Ideas

Scan & Funnel

Resourceful Mind

Look Out

Identify Gaps

Align Available Resources

Look Inside

ATTITUDE ALTERATION

Behavioral Change

Living Core Values

MAD in Action

ATTITUDE ALTERATION

Behavioral Change

Strip off your negativity and toss it away. It only keeps you down and out, unable to rise up from the ranks of mediocrity and unwilling to do anything about it. Changing your attitude is a continuous process. It takes conscious effort and discipline. Think of it as being like putting on new clothes every day. You look better and feel healthier. Your outlook improves and along with it comes the desire to be the best you can be. You become an agent of change, infecting others around you with your passion, enthusiasm, commitment, and determination.

Attitude alteration is all about discarding a negative outlook and taking on a positive mindset and character.

ATTITUDE ALTERATION

Behavioral Change

"I won't change it! There is no other way to do it! This is the best I can do!"

vs

"If there is a better way to produce better results, please guide me and I will do it."

"It's not my fault! I'm born this way!"

vs

"I'm sorry about the mistake. I will work on it and improve. I will not repeat the mistake."

NMA

PMA

VS

"I always fail"

vs

"I will do my best! I won't give up!"

"Why change? I detest change! Take it or leave it!"

vs

"I will change if that will help to improve and develop my character."

"These customers are unreasonable and demanding! I dislike serving them! I don't care if they don't come again!"

vs

"I must find out why these customers are not happy. There must be some other ways that I can do to delight them and make them my loyal customers!"

36

ATTITUDE ALTERATION

Behavioral Change

"My boss is always
picking on me!
She is never satisfied with my
performance!
I give up!"

vs

"I must learn to understand
and appreciate my boss'
expectations of my work.
I must not only meet my job
function but deliver more.
I'm sure I can learn from her!"

"I'm not as lucky as her!
She is successful because she is born
into a rich family!
Obviously, she can have everything!"

vs

"I know I can do it even with the little
resources I have. I will work hard
and multiply what I have now.
Perseverance and diligence will surely
reward me, one day!"

NMA

PMA

VS

"Why trouble yourself
to make a difference!"

vs

"I will take the effort
to make a difference in
my life and in the lives
of others!"

"I know everything!
There is nothing else to learn!"

vs

"I will keep on learning and
increasing my knowledge and
understanding. Even in mistakes,
I learn. Learning makes me wiser.
It enriches my life."

A person with a positive mental attitude (PMA) views the
same scenario, problem or challenge from a completely
different perspective than one with a negative mental
attitude (NMA). The PMA person is likely to find the solution,
while the NMA person gives up, often without even trying.

37

ATTITUDE ALTERATION

Behavioral Change

PROVERBS on NMA and PMA:

NMA ➪ Pride comes before destruction.
PMA ➪ Humility produces greatness and gains honor.

NMA ➪ Fools despise learning and discipline, and calamity overtakes them.
PMA ➪ The wise listen and add to their learning; attaining wisdom and understanding words of insight, and acquiring a disciplined and prudent life.

NMA ➪ The unfaithful are ruined by their duplicity.
PMA ➪ The integrity of the upright guides them to life and reaps a sure reward.

NMA ➪ A ruthless man brings trouble on himself.
PMA ➪ A kind-hearted man gains respect.

NMA ➪ A harsh word stirs up anger and bitterness.
PMA ➪ A gentle answer turns away wrath and brings healing.

NMA ➪ A quick-tempered man speaks recklessly and stirs up dissension. He exposes his folly.
PMA ➪ He who refreshes others will himself be refreshed and finds goodwill.

38

ATTITUDE ALTERATION

Living Core Values

We often hear people say this of their colleague: "He's a great co-worker but a lousy friend to have." Creating and maintaining a healthy and positive office environment requires more than just a change in attitude and behavior at work. The change must be holistic and extend across every aspect of your life. You should embrace core values like the desire to care and share, passion, respect, courage, compassion, commitment, trustworthiness, integrity, humility, and responsibility—not only at work, but also at play and at home. Only then can you truly leave behind such negative feelings and emotions as hostility, resentment, insecurity, anger, and jealousy. Over time, these noble values would become an integral part of your character.

MAD in Action

ATTITUDE ALTERATION

Living Core Values

Define and instil critical core values that will transform your being

Values must form daily habits and practices

Living the core values must produce the desired results: high positive growth and virtuous lifestyle

Consciously put effort to live the values daily

Values become natural part of your being, character, and behavior

Developing living core values requires a step-by-step approach. You need to first identify those values before making a concerted effort to practice them every day wherever you are. Over time, it would be in your nature to behave this way.

MAD in Action

DESIRE DISTINCTION

Spirit of
Excellence

Heart Set for
Positive Change

MAD in Action

DESIRE DISTINCTION

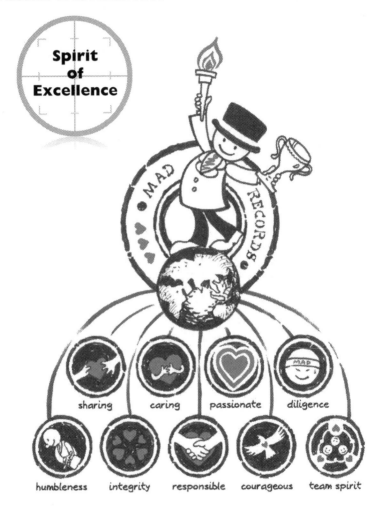

Spirit of Excellence

sharing   caring   passionate   diligence

humbleness   integrity   responsible   courageous   team spirit

Changing the way you think and behave won't result in positive growth if you don't instil a drive and desire for distinction. It would be like climbing Mount Everest, only to stop midway instead of going all the way to the peak. To excel in everything you do is the icing on the cake once you have taken the steps to embrace **MADBiz**. You must have an unshakeable spirit of excellence and your heart set for positive change.

42

MAD in Action

DESIRE DISTINCTION

Spirit
of
Excellence

What is the **Spirit of Excellence**?

It is birthed and cultivated in the innermost being. It is not just about being intellectual. It is almost spiritual, rising from the depths of your soul and from your intense desire to attain the best possible, the most excellent and satisfying result. This burning desire manifests itself through your behavior and way of living. This zealous spirit within you shapes your way of thinking and doing. Almost everything that flows out from your inner being is striving to achieve brilliance and distinction.

There are several important ingredients that contribute to the Spirit of Excellence.

However, I will only emphasize three core ingredients without which one cannot attain the Spirit of Excellence.

MAD in Action

DESIRE DISTINCTION

The **Spirit of Excellence** is a value that can be inculcated in each and every individual, irrespective of rank, status, or job description. It raises your work ethic to the highest level and drives your growth and development. An organization where every employee—from the very top to the bottom-most tier—holds on to this mindset is an organization that produces the most remarkable results and achieves even what seems unattainable.

44

DESIRE DISTINCTION

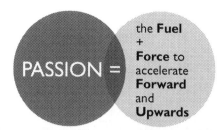

An essential and vital ingredient that accompanies the spirit of excellence is **Passion for Results**.

My definition of passion is intensity of desire that triumphs over any form of suffering or hardship, in pursuit of that burning desire.

Passion spawns energy and strength, determination and courage, ideas and resources.

Passion breeds determination. It fuels endurance and perseverance. It provides the zeal to face and overcome all challenges. Passion is infectious, with the ability to spread to those around you.

Passion gives you the willpower, endurance, and unwavering focus to pursue your targets in record time. Focus is a key in achieving excellence, because it harnesses the energy to pursue the desired goal. It gives you clarity as it removes distractions, so you can concentrate and be selective or discerning in your pursuit of the targets.

Passion drives competency. The fervor and zeal to improve oneself will overcome all challenges.

Passion ignites sparks for other team members to catch the fire and pursue the same courses of action.

Passion gives the additional force to scale upwards to possess the best possible excellent results. It provides the fuel to speed up or pick up the pace to achieve the desired results in record time.

Passion in a person is like fuel in a car or an airplane. It burns hot and deep within to generate the force necessary to drive you forward and upwards.

45

DESIRE DISTINCTION

Spirit of Excellence

Another key ingredient is **Courage to Soar.**

Being passionate but afraid to overcome situations or not daring to leap forward or to soar high above the norm will not lead you anywhere!

Courage lends the strength to go where one has never gone before. It fortifies you in the face of even the toughest challenges and most extreme adversities.

"Courage is doing what you're afraid to do. There can be no courage unless you're scared." — Eddie Rickenbacker

"It is courage, courage, courage, that raises the blood of life to crimson splendour. Live bravely and present a brave front to adversity!" — Horace

"Last, but by no means least, courage—moral courage, the courage of one's convictions, the courage to see things through. The world is in a constant conspiracy against the brave. It's the age-old struggle—the roar of the crowd on one side and the voice of your conscience on the other." — Douglas MacArthur

---

DESIRE DISTINCTION

Another important ingredient is **Humbleness to Learn.**

Learning is everyday, without an end. In every situation, good or bad, success or failure, there is always something to learn. A person who thinks that he has learned everything about life and everything else is a proud and foolish person. He will never achieve excellence in his life. A person only stops learning when he dies.

Humbleness allows you to learn. It prevents you from being arrogant and complacent. By subscribing to the concept of lifelong learning, you can continue to grow in mind and spirit.

A person who always keeps his mind open to gain more knowledge and has keenness on developing a learning culture is a wise person. However knowledgeable or smart or wealthy we are, we must have the humility to be taught, disciplined, and to learn from people from all walks of life.

A successful sportsman or musician is taught and disciplined by his coach or tutor. He has to learn to submit in humility to the guidance and teaching of his coach or tutor.

A corporate high flyer is up on his career ladder because he learns from his superiors.

A person who is humble in spirit will gain more favor, respect, and support from others. This will enable the person to achieve excellence in greater measure and pace.

To attain the spirit of excellence, we must grow in humbleness, to be teachable and to learn.

47

DESIRE DISTINCTION

Spirit of Excellence

Passion for Results **+** Courage to Soar **+** Humbleness to learn

By generating a passion for results and building courage to soar while remaining humble enough to learn, you will carry with you a Spirit of Excellence that leads you to victory in whatever you do.

"If a man is called to be a street sweeper,
He should sweep streets even as
Michelangelo painted, or
Beethoven composed music, or
Shakespeare wrote poetry.
He should sweep streets so well
That all the host of heaven and earth
Will pause to say,
Here lived a great street sweeper
Who did his job well."
— Martin Luther King, Jr.

48

DESIRE DISTINCTION

If you believe you can do it and feel that it is possible, then just do it!

A positive heart and a positive mind will surely lead to positive growth.

When you're in a race, natural ability and physical power can only take you so far. Often, it comes down to whether you have the heart to overcome self-doubt and other obstacles in your path to surge and stay ahead.

> "To put the world right in order, we must first put the nation in order; to put the nation in order, we must first put the family in order; to put the family in order, we must first cultivate our personal life; we must first set our hearts right." - Confucius

49

MAD in Action

DESIRE DISTINCTION

Heart Set
for Positive
Change

$$(\boxed{+}_{Emotions}) + (\boxed{+}_{Thinking})$$

$$= \boxed{+}_{Action}$$

A heart set for positive change comes from a positive spirit. The spirit gives birth to the strength and steadfastness for the soul to take on the challenge for positive change. The spirit knows the goal and purpose for pursuing the change.

The soul comprises the mind (thinking), the emotions (feelings), and the will (action).

DESIRE DISTINCTION

Heart Set for Positive Change

$$\left(\bigoplus Heart\right) + \left(\bigoplus Mind\right) = \bigoplus Growth$$

A heart set for positive change is determined and committed to persevere and overcome obstacles and reap the benefit from changes to achieve positive growth.

> Without continual growth and progress, such words as improvement, achievement, and success have no meaning.
> - Benjamin Franklin

51

My MAD notes

M – Mind Modification
A – Attitude Alteration
D – Desire Distinction

Familiarity leads to complacency, preventing us from doing things better and achieving goals faster.

MAD in Action

[Learning is everyday, without an end. In every situation, good or bad, success or failure, there is always something to learn.]

_____

_____

_____

_____

_____

_____

_____

_____

[However knowledgeable or smart or wealthy we are,
we must have the humility to be taught, disciplined, and
to learn from people from all walks of life.]

MAD in Action

are you mad?

Part II

MAD
@WORKPLACE

➤ **L**eadership's **R**ole
➤ **T**eam's **G**oal

LEADERSHIP'S ROLE

M – **M**aneuver Change
Message Consistency
Mentoring and Role Modelling

A – **A**lignment Setting
Achievement Driven

D – **D**efine Work Culture and Climate
Develop Dynamism in Workplace

MAD in Action

A leader is like the conductor of an orchestra. While each individual has his or her own talent and specific role, it is the leader who provides the direction so that they can all work in concert, rather than in isolation. Only then can they gel together as a team to produce outstanding results.

A leader provides the vision and the inspiration for his team. A leader does not need to have the loudest voice but should have the most visible presence. A leader need not bark orders but can instead coach and guide. Above all, a leader leads by example.

57

LEADERSHIP'S ROLE

Maneuver Change

To stay on the same course irrespective of the circumstances is a recipe for disaster. Change is not only healthy but also necessary when the situation calls for it. Change opens the door to new opportunities that can contribute to better results and higher yields. The leader's role is to steer the organization in the right direction to take advantage of potential prospects. The leader is responsible for leading the change as well as helping others to adapt to the adjustment.

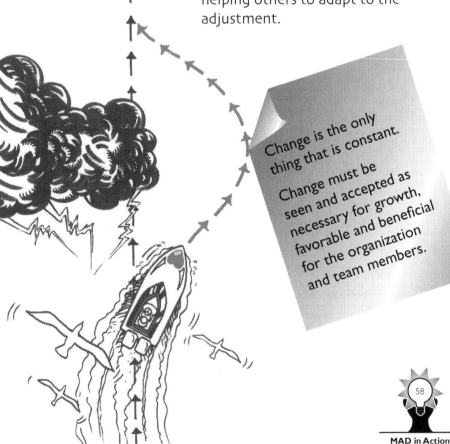

Change is the only thing that is constant.

Change must be seen and accepted as necessary for growth, favorable and beneficial for the organization and team members.

58

MAD in Action

LEADERSHIP'S ROLE

Maneuver Change

Leaders must lead the change—business structure, system, policies, workflow; goals and strategies; work culture and climate.

Establish joint responsibility and accountability. Empower and delegate authority to team leaders.

Direct, align, and coach the team if and when it goes off-track and loses focus on the purpose and goals of the change.

For change to succeed and achieve its goals

Provide prescriptions for team members to manage and adapt to changes.

Closely monitor and follow through the development stages of changes.

59

MAD in Action

Leadership's Role

Maneuver Change

Change may be healthy, but if not managed and implemented properly, it can also bring about chaos and cause disruption, leading to frustration and discontentment among employees.

For change to be effective, leaders must show the way. They must lead the change, whether it is to the business structure, the system in place, the corporate policies, or the workflow. Leaders must set new goals and outline the necessary strategies. They must define the work culture and climate to achieve the goals.

Leading the change also means that the leader has to guide others to manage and adapt to the changes. Here, the leader must highlight what team members have to do so they can grasp their respective roles to bring about the change.

Change is only possible if others get on board. Leaders should delegate responsibility and with it, accountability down the line. Empower your staff to encourage cooperation.

The next task is to track progress at every stage, to ensure team members are able to keep up. If anyone falls behind or goes off-track, it is the leader's responsibility to bring them back on course.

LEADERSHIP'S ROLE

Maneuver Change

Leaders must remain focused on the purpose and plans of the intended change, even when faced with objections, obstacles, or challenges.

When and where needed, go back to the drawing board, but only with the intention to draw or revise strategies, tactical plans, or resources. The purpose and goals of the change should remain unchanged.

If purpose and goals have to be changed, these may indicate that they were not well thought through from the very beginning.

Leaders' behavior and actions must be consistent with the change called for. There must not be duplicity and inconsistency, for this will lead to distrust, loss of confidence and integrity between management and staff. The changed plan will fail or will not produce the desired results.

LEADERSHIP'S ROLE

Message Consistency

A leader is responsible for ensuring that messages are clear and consistent and that they are efficiently communicated to the entire organization. You must master your message, particularly when it concerns your organization's vision, mission, and objectives. Messages must be communicated and explained as to their purpose and intentions. This will ensure that everyone is heading in the same direction.

Always lead by example, especially in influencing plans and strategies. Once you are able to gain buy-in from team members, they will naturally be committed to achieve the objectives and perform at the highest level.

In contrast, an inconsistent message would create confusion, upset focus, and dampen confidence and enthusiasm. This, in turn, can lead to inconsistent results, due to the poor performance and low productivity of team members.

62

LEADERSHIP'S ROLE

The advice "stay on message" applies as much to the world of business as it does to the realm of politics. If every member of the team is on the same wavelength when it comes to understanding the organization's goals and plans, they would be of one mind, one heart. But if a team member on the grapevine strays off message, the line would be broken, and messages would be mistaken, misunderstood, or misdirected.

LEADERSHIP'S ROLE

Message Consistency

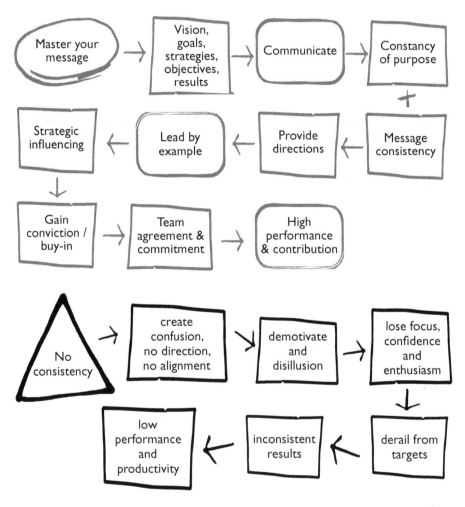

Master your message → Vision, goals, strategies, objectives, results → Communicate → Constancy of purpose

Strategic influencing ← Lead by example ← Provide directions ← Message consistency

Gain conviction / buy-in → Team agreement & commitment → High performance & contribution

No consistency → create confusion, no direction, no alignment → demotivate and disillusion → lose focus, confidence and enthusiasm → derail from targets ← inconsistent results ← low performance and productivity

64

LEADERSHIP'S ROLE

Mentoring and Role Modelling

Effective leaders do not merely develop a vision and inspire their team members. They also have a responsibility to cultivate the next generation of leaders. This is where Mentoring and Role Modelling come in.

Leaders should guide their team members to perform their tasks and pass down their knowledge, skills, and experience. They should become the role model of leadership by leading by example, as well as coaching and delegating.

Leaders must not only practice what they preach, but more importantly, they should preach what they are practicing! "Walk the talk, talk the walk!"

65

MAD in Action

LEADERSHIP'S ROLE

Mentoring and Role Modelling

Mentors help shape the character and competency of their mentees, empowering them by delegating certain responsibilities that, in turn, cultivate a sense of ownership and shared accountability to strive for the common goals as a team.

Mentors don't just dictate; they also walk the talk and live the values, to act as a source of inspiration and motivation. They are engaged together with their mentees and are result-focused and achievement-driven.

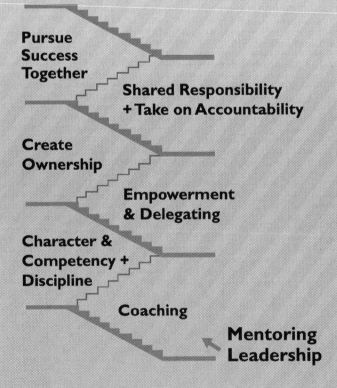

Celebrate Achievements

Pursue Success Together

Shared Responsibility + Take on Accountability

Create Ownership

Empowerment & Delegating

Character & Competency + Discipline

Coaching

Mentoring Leadership

66

MAD in Action

LEADERSHIP'S ROLE

Mentoring and Role Modelling

achievement-driven

↑

results-focused

↑

intellectually & emotionally engaged

↑

inspire & motivate

↑

leading by serving + living the values

↑

walk the talk

Mentoring Leadership

67

MAD in Action

LEADERSHIP'S ROLE

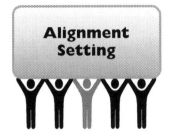

Alignment Setting

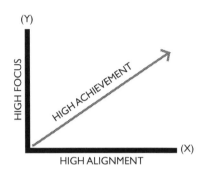

High achievement is only possible if the team or organization is always aligned and focused on the goals. It requires a high-focused direction and high commitment that will then lead to high productivity and high growth.

MAD in Action

LEADERSHIP'S ROLE

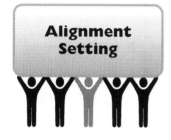

Alignment Setting

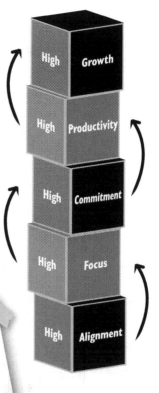

High Growth

High Productivity

High Commitment

High Focus

High Alignment

It's the leadership's role and responsibility to renew the team's perspective and understanding of the organization's vision and goals, their roles and contributions, and to re-align their focus.

When the team has wrong or displaced focus, they will not be able to see clearly. Their vision is blurred because their focus is not aligned to the organization's vision. Align and position their thoughts, perceptions, behavior, and contributions, in order to reach the organization's desired destination in record time.

LEADERSHIP'S ROLE

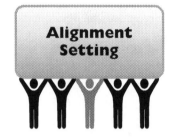

Alignment
Setting

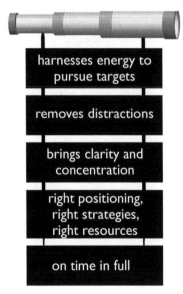

harnesses energy to pursue targets

removes distractions

brings clarity and concentration

right positioning, right strategies, right resources

on time in full

Importance of Focusing

Keeping all members of the team focused in the same direction at all times is vital in achieving your targets. It doesn't make a difference whether you're in the military or a corporation—it's all the same. When your team can work and think as one, the members can complement each other's knowledge, skills, and experience. They are less susceptible to "doing their own thing" and less prone to distractions. It is the leader's role and responsibility to bring clarity and concentration to the team so that they can stay on the right path for the right positioning with the right strategies and right resources. Attention!

70

LEADERSHIP'S ROLE

Achievement Driven

You'll often find that the path to success is never a straight and easy line from point A to point B. If it were, what would be the fun? As a leader, you may have to lead your team through a path littered with obstacles and fraught with potential hazards. Under your guidance, team members would have to keep their eye on the target while solving problems along the way.

Reaching your goals makes each member a champion and you a champion of champions!

MAD in Action

LEADERSHIP'S ROLE

Achievement Driven

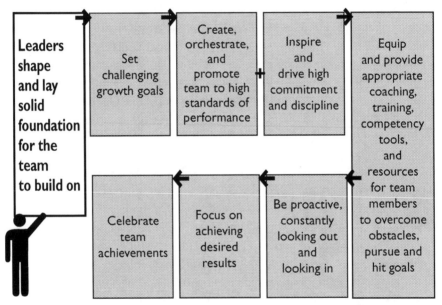

Leaders shape and lay solid foundation for the team to build on	Set challenging growth goals	Create, orchestrate, and promote team to high standards of performance	Inspire and drive high commitment and discipline	Equip and provide appropriate coaching, training, competency tools, and resources for team members to overcome obstacles, pursue and hit goals
	Celebrate team achievements	Focus on achieving desired results	Be proactive, constantly looking out and looking in	

The ability of the team or organization in meeting its goals rests on the leader's shoulders. Leaders shape and build a solid foundation for the team to fulfil its targets. The leader must set challenging goals, stretch expectations and measurements so that they will drive high performance. Leaders must make efforts to align clear expectations and goals with the team before inspiring their enthusiasm and marshalling the performance of the team in every aspect of their planning and operation. Leaders also start the ball rolling to celebrate team achievements.

72

MAD in Action

LEADERSHIP'S ROLE

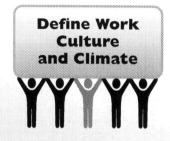

Define Work Culture and Climate

The contrast between a healthy and an unhealthy work environment can be quite obvious the minute you step into the respective offices. The very air is different! At one end of the spectrum are cheerful and relaxed employees who are ever ready to offer you a smile. They have an air of confidence and do everything at a brisk pace. At the other end, all you get are glum and sour looks from people who tend to ignore you by burying their faces in their computer screens. Work seems to be tedious, and there is little interaction and conversation throughout.

73

LEADERSHIP'S ROLE

Define Work Culture and Climate

Examine, identify, and understand underlying issues affecting work culture and climate

▼

Tailor solutions and take corrective measures

▼

Define critical core values that are integral to achieving your vision

▼

Consistently lead by living the values

▼

Inspire and be the change

▼

Reflect and shape desired work culture and climate in all work plans and activities

▼

Acknowledge and celebrate high-performing staff with good character and competencies

The type of culture and kind of climate at any workplace comes down to the leader. Leaders have to constantly test the air, so as to better understand the issues that affect the work environment. This enables you to take remedial actions and replace negative influences with positive ones. Inspire and shape the way your team members go about planning and implementing your vision. Engage their hearts and minds, and connect with them on a personal level so that they will internalize your vision and make it theirs.

74

MAD in Action

LEADERSHIP'S ROLE

Define Work Culture and Climate

Instil a learning culture and a positive working climate. Inspire team leadership to create shared responsibility, and equip them to take charge and accountability for building organizational capability and performance.

Where there are grievances or disruptions within the organization (people, operations, or systems), do not delay in tackling them. Take ownership and responsibility to manage them. When needed, take immediate actions to remove any negative or obstructive elements in the organization.

Leaders do not demonstrate behavior or employ strategies and tactics that are contradictory or inconsistent with the organization's vision and values.

Leaders must create an atmosphere of integrity, accountability, respect, and stability in order to build a strong, healthy, and successful team.

MAD in Action

LEADERSHIP'S ROLE

A dynamic team is always one step ahead of its competitors and sometimes of its own expectations. In this team, every member seems to operate as if by remote control to execute and complete his or her specific task with a high degree of application and enthusiasm. Each member's effort fits in nicely with that of the others, and what you get at the end of the day is a final product that reflects pride and perfection. A team devoid of dynamism may only be putting the first pieces together when all is said and done.

76

LEADERSHIP'S ROLE

Develop Dynamism in Workplace

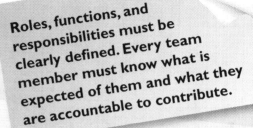

Roles, functions, and responsibilities must be clearly defined. Every team member must know what is expected of them and what they are accountable to contribute.

Career advancement is, after all, an important factor if you are to maintain dynamism at the workplace. Once leaders and their teams have outgrown their respective roles, it is time to introduce new challenges to provide opportunities for personal growth. In such cases, it is preferable to re-assign them in a higher position with greater responsibilities or shift them laterally to other projects that offer a different set of roles and parameters.

However, do not attempt to place an individual in a position of responsibility for which he is not prepared, equipped, or suited. Regardless of how competent the staff member was in his previous position, he may sometimes be unable to deliver the same level of effectiveness and efficiency when he is placed in the wrong position. Eventually he ends up frustrated, overworked, and underproductive as he is unable to fulfill the demands or adjust to his new role and function. He becomes ineffective, not because he is a poor performer but because the shoes given to him are far too large for his feet. A significant gap exists between his current capability and the dimensions of his new position.

77

LEADERSHIP'S ROLE

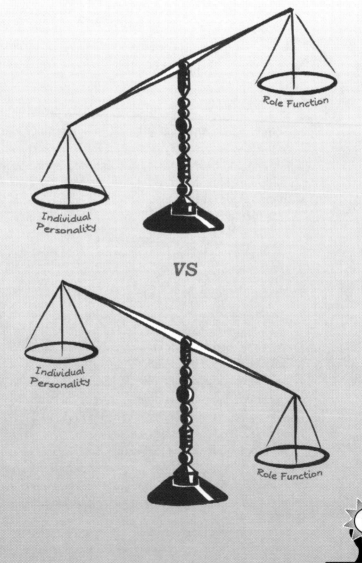

MAD in Action

LEADERSHIP'S ROLE

Develop Dynamism in Workplace

There must be a balance between the staff's job function and their individual personality.

While leaders work towards building the competency of every team member, however, we must avoid creating a permanent situation where the personality of the individual becomes bigger or overwhelms the job function or role description. It is a case where the personality is more important (weightier) than the job nature itself. Without that personality, the job crumbles!

In such cases, the individual needs to be shifted to another position to match his or her growing influence and strength. If this is not done, it will later lead to the individual being dissatisfied with the limited or constrained growth. The individual may also become the focal attention of success and pride, which if not attended to, will lead to an unhealthy work climate, where other members feel they are less important and not recognized for their achievements. They will be disconnected and disengaged with the management.

79

Leadership's Role

M – **M**aneuver Change
Message Consistency
Mentoring and Role Modelling

A – **A**lignment Setting
Achievement Driven

D – **D**efine Work Culture & Climate
Develop **D**ynamism in Workplace

My MAD notes

[
Reaching your goals makes each member a champion
and you a champion of champions!
]

-----

*Leaders shape and build a solid foundation for the team
to fulfil its targets.*

are you mad?

TEAM'S GOAL

M – Maximize Team Spirit
Manage Team Dynamics

A – Attitude and **A**ptitude
Acceleration and **A**ltitude

D – Design Fun@Work
Drive **D**ifferentiations

MAD in Action

Team's Goal

Like all team sports, soccer revolves around teamwork. While players are assigned set positions with specific roles, it is how they play together that will decide whether the team wins or loses. The better teams are always greater than the sum of their parts. Successful teams show greater understanding, better communication and coordination among the players. The ones that play together and for each other score the best results. After all, they have a common goal!

MAD in Action

TEAM'S GOAL

Maximize Team Spirit

The next time you see a line of ants, stop and take a moment to watch them at work. Few species can match the sort of team spirit and teamwork you see among them. If you look closely, you will find that there are different teams doing different things. Some forage for food, while others work to build, repair, and reinforce their nest. They all have the same objective: to keep their queen fed, safe, and secure.

TEAM'S GOAL

Maximize Team Spirit

How many employees does it take to change the light?

It normally takes one, but if it's too high to reach, then perhaps it's a job for more than one! Teams are more than just a collection of individuals. By pooling their strengths and skills and working together, team members can reach their goals easier, much faster, and more efficiently than if they were to work in isolation.

Team spirit is vital for high achievement, for it brings individual members together to work, play, and win as a team. Here, personal agendas are replaced by a single vision and common objectives.

"We" replaces "I" in their effort to reach the goals and reap the benefits. Team members share responsibility and accountability in an atmosphere where they accept each other for their differences, strengths, and weaknesses.

The team that plays well together then toasts their victories as one.

86

MAD in Action

TEAM'S GOAL

Manage Team Dynamics

"As iron sharpens iron, so one man sharpens another." (Proverbs 27:17)

Managing a team is like a juggling act. You need to master the art of creating and maintaining your team dynamics so that members can tap into their potential to grow. At the same time, you need to match each individual's strengths and weaknesses with their roles and responsibilities. Only then can they support one another so that as a team, they can move in the same direction to reach the common goals.

TEAM'S GOAL

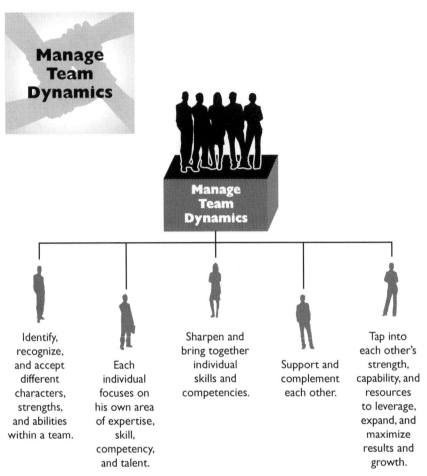

Manage Team Dynamics

| Identify, recognize, and accept different characters, strengths, and abilities within a team. | Each individual focuses on his own area of expertise, skill, competency, and talent. | Sharpen and bring together individual skills and competencies. | Support and complement each other. | Tap into each other's strength, capability, and resources to leverage, expand, and maximize results and growth. |

The first task in building and managing a team is to identify, recognize, and accept that no two members are alike in their characters, strengths, and abilities. Assign them tasks that best suit their specific mind sets and skill sets. Focus their attention on honing their capabilities in support of each other. Then, as a team, they would be able to complement each other to maximize results and growth.

MAD in Action

Team's Goal

Manage Team Dynamics

While we recognize, acknowledge, and celebrate outstanding individuals, it must not be personality-driven. Ultimately it is the collaboration or the gatherings and intertwining of the dynamics of every individual team member that makes a strong, outstanding, winning team.

The staff represents the organization; they are the face and ambassador of the organization.

TEAM'S GOAL

Attitude and Aptitude

WORLD RECORD!

You need balance as much as strength in weightlifting. Strength enables you to lift the weights, while balance lets you hold it together without toppling to one side. Similarly, in a team, each member should have these attributes—attitude and aptitude, character and competency—to carry their part.

They need to have the right attitude to display commitment and determination; the required aptitude to fulfil the requirements of the role; the desired character to be part of a team; and the necessary competency to perform the task. These attributes must go hand-in-hand as a package.

90

TEAM'S GOAL

Attitude and Aptitude

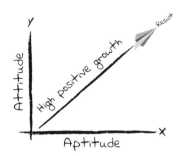

The right attitude and aptitude will lead you to achieve high positive growth.

Create a climate that inspires positive attitude and growth by instilling team members to believe, think, talk, and live positively through their words, actions, priorities and performance.

Cultivate a positive mental attitude approach in your organization by developing positive mindset through living some key core values daily. Consciously drive the core values that you have introduced to challenge their mental attitudes, as this can change their behavior and performance level. It requires conscious effort in the beginning to practice the values, but over time, they may become a natural part of their personality and behavior. This will enhance their competency levels to deliver the desired results.

> Integrity is an essential ingredient in character, and without it, over time, would result in the loss of respect, trust, and commitment from people.
>
> An employee who is highly competent but who does not possess good character is not worth keeping.

Competency with poor character = short-term gains, not enduring results.

91

MAD in Action

TEAM'S GOAL

Attitude and Aptitude

"Life is 10 % what you make it and 90% how you take it." —Irving Berlin

"Character is like a tree, and reputation is like a shadow. The shadow is what we think of it; the tree is the real thing." —Abraham Lincoln

"A man of character will make himself worthy of any position he is given." —Mahatma Gandhi

"I have a dream that my four little children will one day live in a nation where they will not be judged by the colour of their skin but by the content of their character." —Martin Luther King, Jr.

92

TEAM'S GOAL

Acceleration
and
Altitude

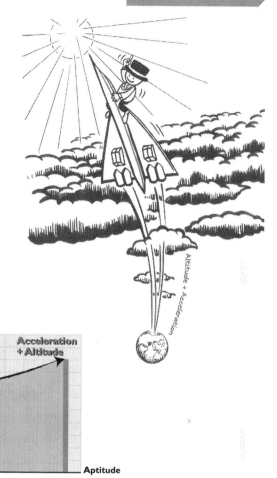

The Four A's of success

Attitude + Aptitude ⇨ Acceleration + Altitude

It doesn't take much to figure out that flying high requires acceleration to gain altitude and soar above the clouds. Altitude to reach the heights of success and acceleration to do so efficiently are only possible in an individual or organization that has a positive attitude and the correct aptitude. These are the Four A's of success in which attitude and aptitude are necessary to attain acceleration and altitude.

93

TEAM'S GOAL

Design Fun @Work

Enjoy what you do. Be excited about your work. Look forward to work.
Be happy working! Your work is your passion.

Generating fun@work lets you and your team members work hard and play hard.

A fun workplace, along with stimulating work, creates the right atmosphere for your mind and body to function at the highest level. This translates to better-quality contributions by everyone on the way to achieving positive results.

TEAM'S GOAL

**Design Fun
@Work**

Most people spend more of their waking hours at work than they do at home. While many people view the workplace as their second home, some even proclaim it is, in fact, their first home!

Lighten up the workplace by putting up heart-warming and creative decorations during festive seasons, or set a theme or slogan to reinforce the vision or core values of the organization. Celebrate achievements or develop a creative program that motivates and rewards those who conscientiously display and work toward creating a better environment and work culture.

Work environments should offer a balance by including some form of leisure and entertainment to take the edge off employees for their hard work and determination. Opportunities for fun and games at the workplace go a long way to rejuvenate tired minds and refresh aching bodies so they can continue to generate higher productivity and greater successes. After all, all work and no play is not what the doctor ordered!

MAD in Action

TEAM'S GOAL

Drive Differentiation

When we look at a forest, each of us may have a different idea of what to use it for. Some may see it as a source of wood and timber for housing construction. Others may want to turn it into a recreational park, while a third group may only think of catching and caging the birds!

MAD in Action

TEAM'S GOAL

Drive Differentiation

In business, we are naturally different from our competitors in what we offer to consumers. Our products and services have their own unique selling point.

It is the team's key task to identify what differentiates your business from others. This team decision could determine the success or failure of your business plan.

97

MAD in Action

TEAM'S GOAL

Drive Differentiation

Albert Einstein said, "The significant problems we face cannot be solved at the same level of thinking we were at when we created them."

Similarly, we cannot attain extraordinary results if we remain at the same level of thinking and working as now. It is a given that if you stick to the same, you will only get more of the same.

Be inspirational. Engage your heart, energize your mind and challenge your creative spirit to unlock your creativity and innovative mind. Throw in new ideas, and you just may be surprised by the results.

Generate different results by thinking and acting differently!

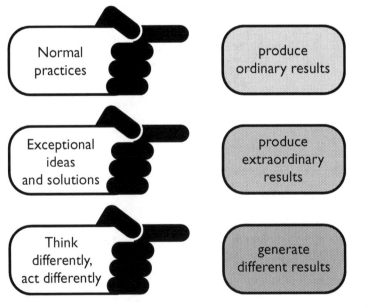

Normal practices	produce ordinary results
Exceptional ideas and solutions	produce extraordinary results
Think differently, act differently	generate different results

98

TEAM'S GOAL

Drive Differentiation

Do not settle and be complacent with ordinary ways of doing things.

Work from a different platform in order to see from a different perspective. Wear different lenses of perception. Put aside biases or prejudice. Be open-minded to all possible ideas and solutions.

The source of your point of differentiation can come from products, attributes or solutions, brands, services, pricing, distribution or product accessibility, or from creating customers' experience.

Probe yourself:
"What is so special about my business?
Why should my customers come to me and not to my competitors?
How and what do I want my customers to remember me by?
How else can I delight my customers?
What else is possible to ensure growth opportunities are realized?"

These differentiations will set you apart from your competition.

Team's Goal

M – **M**aximize Team Spirit
Manage Team Dynamics
Mentoring and Role **M**odelling

A – **A**ttitude and **A**ptitude
Acceleration and **A**ltitude

D – **D**esign Fun@Work
Drive **D**ifferentiations

My MAD notes

MAD in Action

Build character by living your core values

Managing a team is like a juggling act.
You need to master the art of creating and maintaining
your team dynamics so that members can tap
into their potential to grow.

MAD in Action

are you mad?

Part III

MAD
@ MARKETPLACE

➤ Frame Work of **MAD**
➤ Strategic Execution of **MAD**

Frame Work of MAD

M – Mind Map

A – Aligned Actions

D – Desired Results

104

FRAME WORK OF MAD

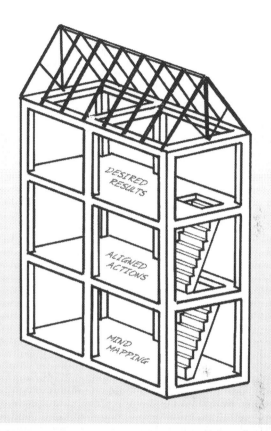

How do you build a multi-storey house? First, lay the foundation, and then build the frame work floor by floor, so that each floor can support the construction of the next. The MAD concept follows a similar approach. Start by mind mapping your objectives and goals as well as the resources and actions necessary to achieve them. Follow this up by integrating and aligning your plans, strategies, and execution of actions with the objectives and goals in mind. Then consciously shape your plans to achieve the desired results you want.

FRAME WORK OF MAD

Mind Map

Mind mapping helps you to see how extensive or far-reaching your project can be, the potential results you can achieve, and the deliverables. Keep branching out ideas and solutions and then identify, analyze, select, and execute those that will bring positive growth to your organization.

MAD in Action

Frame Work of MAD

Mind Map

Imagine you can tip your hat and let out all your thought processes. Then arrange them accordingly in a "map" to paint the big picture of what you need to do first, and so on.

Mind mapping is a key building block of **MADBiz**. It is a highly effective method to generate, visualize, structure, and classify ideas as well as to organize your resources, solve problems, and arrive at decisions.

Mind mapping helps to identify areas of priority and where there are gaps that need to be filled.

FRAME WORK OF MAD

Aligned Actions

I'm sure there must have been times when you had to suppress a laugh when someone bowled into the gutter. Bear in mind that it can happen to you too! To achieve a strike, bowlers must align their minds and bodies to deliver the ball in the right direction with the proper speed to knock down all ten pins. Your motor coordination must be perfect so that your eyes, arms, and legs work exactly the way the mind set out to do.

The same principles apply to the world of business. Once you have finalized, confirmed, and are happy with your "map," then the implementation stage comes in. It's action time—the most exciting and critical stage.

You need to align the execution of your plans and strategies to meet your objectives to hit your target, or else you will see your projects going down the drain!

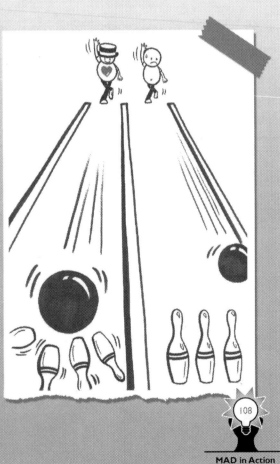

108

FRAME WORK OF MAD

Aligned Actions

Align Strategies + Programs

Constancy of Purpose => meet objectives => exceed targets

If your strategies and programs are aligned with the main purpose, then you are on track toward meeting your objectives and exceeding your targets.

Integrate, pattern, and align all strategies and plans (programs, activities) to be in line with and consistent with the purpose of the project and the organization's vision. Never derail or run off course from the main purpose of the project. Stay focused on achieving the targeted goals. Do not be sidetracked by peripheral issues.

You must:
- know your purpose for executing the strategy
- know your positioning and its relative strength in terms of products, branding, pricing, and all other marketing mix
- know where and how to draw resources to support your project from start to finish
- construct, shape and align all tasks or action plans to be in line with the objectives of the purpose
- regularly monitor progress against timeframes and take immediate corrective measures when and where necessary
- not lose sight of purpose, goals or targets when faced with challenges.

Keep focusing on achieving desired results. Pursue with objectives and goals in mind.

109

MAD in Action

FRAME WORK OF MAD

Aligned Actions

This map helps you to achieve synchronicity in your plans and strategies against the goals and objectives.

How to ALIGN ACTIONS

FOCUS
- Purpose, goals, and end results
- Review results against growth goals

KNOW
- Purpose and goals for executing strategies
- Positioning of products, branding, pricing, market segmentations, etc.
- Project resources

ALIGN
- All tasks/actions must be aligned to objectives of purpose
- Consciously shape or pattern all action plans to achieve desired results
- Regularly monitor progress against timeframes

MAD in Action

FRAME WORK OF MAD

Desired Results

Archers pick their target first before taking into consideration factors like bow elevation, pull strength, and wind direction to chart the path of the arrow to the right spot. MADBiz prescribes a similar approach in business, where the desired results are determined first so that planning and execution can be tailored to aim for the target. This approach deviates from the traditional way of setting targets according to existing capabilities and capacities.

MAD in Action

FRAME WORK OF MAD

Desired Results

Focus your aim at your target. Temporarily park aside all current constraints and issues. Open your mind to consider all possibilities to achieve the ultimate desired results. Focus on desired results, not issues or inabilities.

Once you have identified the list of workable ideas, strategies, and solutions, and then work on it individually by engaging a resourceful mind and alternative thinking to achieve them, while simultaneously managing and overcoming the current constraints, and leverage current resources to maximize their benefits.

Consciously shape the results that you want to achieve.

MAD in Action

Frame Work of MAD

Desired Results

RENEWED MIND

DESIRED RESULTS
THE GOAL

Engage Open & Creative Thinking

goal 1   goal 2   goal 3   goal 4

| Strategies Solutions | Strategies Solutions | Strategies Solutions | Strategies Solutions |

Engage Resourceful Mind & Alternative Thinking

Action Plans

Current Issues

New Plans

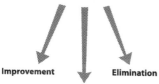

Improvement   Elimination

Alignment

Ideas' selections
Priority
Timing

Resources
Needed

Execution plans
Monitor results

113

MAD in Action

Frame Work of MAD
M – **M**ind **M**ap
A – **A**ligned **A**ctions
D – **D**esired Results

My MAD notes

MAD in Action

[Do not lose sight of purpose, goals, or targets when faced with challenges. Keep focusing on achieving desired results.]

Are the strategies, plans, and programs meeting the objectives and achieving the targeted goals?

MAD in Action

STRATEGIC EXECUTION OF MAD

M – Master Your Message
Maximize and Magnify Resources

A – Articulate "out-of-box" Actions

D – Distinguish, Discern and Be
Disciplined

STRATEGIC EXECUTION OF **MAD**

Every general worth his salt will say that success on the battlefield depends on the effective execution of the battle plan. However brilliant the plan, victory can only be achieved if his tactical commanders and their subordinates can maneuver their forces as outlined and according to schedule.

The MADBiz concept recognizes the fact that poor execution too often torpedoes credible plans. Taking this into consideration, MADBiz places emphasis on dynamic and creative executions of plans to generate the projected outcomes and desired results.

117

STRATEGIC EXECUTION
OF MAD

Master Your Message

Mind to Mind, Heart to Heart!

To achieve the cutting edge in your business, it is critical to make a connection with the customers. It is a battle for the hearts and minds of the customers. Your message must appeal to them intellectually as well as emotionally. It should be tailored in such a way as to capture their attention and appeal to their senses in order to convince them that it is the right choice. Master your message so that it carries the power of influence.

118

STRATEGIC EXECUTION OF MAD

Master Your Message

Every strategy and program must communicate its intended message that is in line with the objectives of the purpose. There are several questions you should ask when evaluating your intended message:

What is the key message that you want to deliver to your targeted audience?

Is the message able to capture the attention and retention of the audience and induce them to act as intended?

What makes you special and different from all your competitors that customers should choose to listen to you?

Is your message worthy and meaningful, and does it give them a good reason to pause, listen to your message, and act on it?

What is your competitive edge?

How does your point of differentiation benefit your customers?

Does it provide solutions to your customers' needs?

What is the desired result of the execution?

Will the execution achieve its purpose?

119

MAD in Action

STRATEGIC EXECUTION OF MAD

Master Your Message

Master the message of what you want to communicate, and emphasize your point of differentiation. Communicate your message persuasively and convincingly to your customers' hearts and minds.

Every player in the market is striving hard to influence and induce their customers to capture a share of their pocket. Ultimately, the most effective strategy that brilliantly engages the emotions of their customers will prevail over all. Emotional engagement plays a vital role in your customers' decision-making.

Always establish close connections with your customers. Constantly touch base with people who contribute to your business. Do not neglect other personnel from within your customers' organization that influence the buying decision, or have a say or a hand in your service of products. The storekeepers or warehouse (logistic) manager are often a valuable source of reliable information. You must know them!

120

STRATEGIC EXECUTION OF MAD

Maximize & Magnify Resources

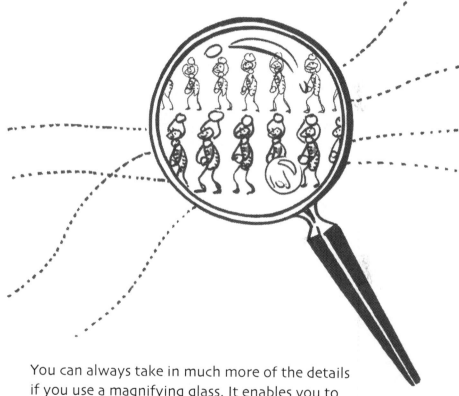

You can always take in much more of the details if you use a magnifying glass. It enables you to examine and identify things that you had missed or overlooked.

"Take a magnifying glass" to your business and see whether you are tapping the full potential of your resources or simply letting them go to waste.

MAD in Action

STRATEGIC EXECUTION OF MAD

Maximize & Magnify Resources

Do not undermine or underestimate what you are and what you have now. It is what you do with what you have.

Often, we overlook our talents, our capabilities, our resources, and the people around us. Deploy, maximize, and amplify the benefits of your best resources to meet objectives. Use multiple methods or integrate the resources or methods as the basis for deliberating strategies to achieve results.

MAD in Action

STRATEGIC EXECUTION OF MAD

Maximize & Magnify Resources

Be discerning and disciplined with where you invest your energy and resources and in your choices or selections of ideas, plans, people, or resources with which to work.

Employ positive influence strategies to gain support, cooperation, and commitment to grow your business.

Consider positive strategic partnership or collaborations whenever necessary.

MAD in Action

STRATEGIC EXECUTION OF MAD

Maximize & Magnify Resources

Food for Thought

Believe and have confidence that you are able to increase and multiply what you have now. Nothing that you have now is too little for you to multiply. It is how you perceive—if you think you have nothing worthwhile to work on, then you are right; you have nothing. However, if you believe in your capability to reproduce, then everything you work on will be productive and multiply.

$$((10 \times 10 = 100))$$

Goal

$$((10 + 10 = 20))$$ **Current**

Maximize your resources to multiply your results.
In this case, ten and ten need not come up to twenty!

124

MAD in Action

STRATEGIC EXECUTION OF MAD

Articulate "Out-of-Box" Actions

Some of the most mind-blowing innovations around today came from the most unlikely sources, created under the most improbable situations. This is the beauty of creative thinking in searching for "out-of-the-box" ideas.

MAD in Action

Strategic Execution of **MAD**

Articulate "Out-of-Box" Actions

Embrace a world of possibilities in finding solutions and ideas in business as well as other aspects of life. Renovate your (old) way of thinking. Step out of the boundaries that you have set. Look outside yourself! Renew your perspective! Expand your paradigm. Move away from your fixed ways of doing things that limit your capabilities and potential to construct and fashion bold ideas into your plans.

Be prepared to go against standard and traditional practices. But bear in mind that it only becomes an innovative idea if it creates value for your customers.

Food for Thought

If you have the power to create something different from what you have now, what would you create?

126

Strategic Execution of MAD

Articulate "Out-of-Box" Actions

"Out-of-box" ideas need not necessarily be huge or complicated ideas. Many innovative ideas come about from tweaking existing ideas. Often, the effect has been significant and even transformative, offering benefits far beyond what could have been imagined.

"Out-of-the-box" ideas do not have to be entirely original to make waves or impact our lives. They only have to be different and constructive, like how a transformer can generate a higher voltage for a brighter light from the very same frame.

MAD in Action

STRATEGIC EXECUTION OF MAD

Articulate "Out-of-Box" Actions

A view from the top can offer you a fresh take of your tasks and their objectives. Don't always be overly engrossed in the minute details of what you need to do. It is always advisable to step back once in a while and review your plans and strategies, to see whether they are going in the right direction. Often, extraordinary ideas require some changes in the way you conduct your normal business. Occasionally it demands a break in the work flow pattern.

You can sometimes arrive at an out-of-the-box solution by "coming out of your own box" and taking in the bigger picture.

128

STRATEGIC EXECUTION OF MAD

Distinguish, Discern & Be Disciplined

Decide and define what you want to be and how you want your customers to see and perceive you.

Describe or spell out your expectations or what goals you want to achieve in a specified timeframe. Then work towards that identity and deliver the distinguished elements in all your strategies, plans, solutions, and activation programs.

Executions of action plans must be consistent, detailed, seamless, and sharp and reflect the organization's vision and business objectives.

The finesse, style, and method of execution are some key points of differentiation that can position you above the rest.

129

MAD in Action

STRATEGIC EXECUTION OF MAD

Distinguish, Discern & Be Disciplined

Be consistent, and do not compromise on the quality of your differentiation. Be diligent to follow through all effects and initiatives of the differentiation. Work towards a distinctive advantage edge.

Your points of differentiation are your trademark! Your customers choose to buy from you because they believe and have confidence in the features and benefits of your trademark. Only you and your organization can deliver your trademark benefits!

Never compromise on quality, be it products, services, business programs, sales and marketing campaigns, distributions, etc. Never slack or neglect the promises you made to your customers.

It is a very expensive lesson to lose loyal customers.

130

STRATEGIC EXECUTION OF MAD

Distinguish, Discern & Be Disciplined

Do not just meet standards of requirement, but deliver delight and satisfaction to customers.

Remember, the basis or cornerstone of an excellent execution is those who delight their customers beyond what they expect to receive.

Always bear in mind that your customers are your paymasters.

So it certainly pays to delight and surprise them!

MAD in Action

STRATEGIC EXECUTION OF MAD

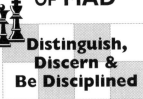

Distinguish, Discern & Be Disciplined

Focus to win the hearts and minds of your customers.

Delight them with good, memorable experiences!

Deliver not just what is required, but what is desired.

Be the best player in your targeted market or category.

Be the most efficient in your point of differentiation.

Be the most sought-after solution provider to your customers.

Be passionate in pursuing and positioning yourself as the "top-of-the-mind" and "core-of-the-heart" of your customers!

MAD in Action

STRATEGIC EXECUTION OF MAD

Distinguish, Discern & Be Disciplined

Wear your long-distance lenses, put on your magnifying glass, and spend some time to read between the lines of your competitors' campaigns and communication programs.

Observe and see through the eyes of your competition to understand and gauge where they are coming from and where they are going.

Focus, discipline, and discernment are very much needed to be practiced in most businesses today.

133

MAD in Action

STRATEGIC EXECUTION OF MAD

Distinguish, Discern & Be Disciplined

Competition is always healthy, as it breeds innovation, raises the quality of your product and service, and produces variety. It allows you to stay on your toes, not only to protect but also expand your market share.

Keep an eye on what your competitors are up to, so that you can plan accordingly to stay ahead. At the same time, remain focused on your targets; your point of differentiation must be incorporated in your message to your customers.

Never orient your strategies around your competitors, as this would put you in the back seat. Instead of being reactive, you should always be proactive and lead.

MAD in Action

STRATEGIC EXECUTION OF MAD

Distinguish, Discern & Be Disciplined

Remain focused on your point of differentiation, and integrate all your work plans to reflect this point of differentiation.

Do not conduct "hit-and-run" campaigns that do not strengthen the attributes of your point of differentiation. Often, we are tempted or challenged by the competition to change our course of directions or core strategies, but a change of plans can disrupt the momentum or positioning of the brand or product.

In some cases, it even alters the purpose or goal of the business plans. (Note: tactical plans can be changed to challenge and overcome impending competition threats.) Alteration of business strategic thrust or purpose or brand value or essence is not advisable, unless it is really warranted and justified in order to seize the future potential. Short-sighted activities or programs are not enduring. They are confusing and will not produce long-lasting results. Nowadays, due to stiff competition, many are led to be reactive to market changes maneuvered by the competition instead of being proactive.

135

MAD in Action

STRATEGIC EXECUTION OF MAD

Distinguish, Discern & Be Disciplined

Knowing the right timing of execution is critical to the success of your plans. Your idea or new product can be very good, or your plans can be perfect, but if you launch your product or plans before the right time (before the seeds are ripe for harvesting), you will not capture or reap the maximum fruit of the harvest.

Likewise, if you execute your launch after the field has been harvested, you miss the prime harvest.

Discernment of timing execution is, therefore, crucial.

Regularly monitor and review progress and results against growth goals.

MAD in Action

STRATEGIC EXECUTION OF MAD

Distinguish, Discern & Be Disciplined

Another key factor to being disciplined is doing homework, i.e., planning and preparation. Great success is often the result of superior preparation, but not excessive neither hasty preparations.

We always hear this advice but we often fail to act on it: "Not planning is planning to fail."

137

STRATEGIC EXECUTION OF MAD

Distinguish, Discern & Be Disciplined

Be deliberate with your projects, from conception of ideas to planning to execution of plans to monitoring results. Let it be well-thought and followed-through.

Constancy of purpose of project must be reflected throughout. Activation programs must be consistent with the agreed positioning of the product or service. Keep and stick to your planned agenda.

Be decisive, and do not make decisions due to pressure tactics from others.

Monitor and review progress to ensure delivery of results.

The 5P's of Executing a Project

Purpose + Positioning + Planning + Preparation + Progress

138

MAD in Action

STRATEGIC EXECUTION OF MAD

Distinguish, Discern & Be Disciplined

Remember:
If your customers perceive you as no different from your competitors, you will lose your market share and will soon be displaced.

To be the preferred supplier to your customers, you must stand out amongst all the other suppliers in your targeted market. What you stand for must be outstanding and distinctive to your target customers.

139

Strategic execution of MAD

M – **M**aster your **M**essage
Maximize and **M**agnify resources

A – **A**rticulate "out-of-box" **A**ctions

D – **D**istinguish, **D**iscern & be **D**isciplined

My MAD notes

It is critical to make a connection with your customers.
It is a battle for the hearts and minds of your customers.

MAD in Action

Be passionate in pursuing and positioning yourself as
the "top-of-the-mind" and "core-of-the-heart" of your customers!

---

*You can sometimes arrive at an out-of-the-box solution by
"coming out of your own box" and taking in the bigger picture.*

MAD in Action

are you mad?

APPENDIX

MAD Keys to Building
A WINNING TEAM
in WINNING CUSTOMERS

Create a healthy climate that emphasizes on good character and high performance. Make it a point to gently remind the team that every job is a self-portrait of the one who does it. Occasionally, I asked my team members this question that I had come across: "Do you want your work to be seen as a masterpiece or a hack-job?" I also would remind them that only unsuccessful people are always asking, "What's in it for me?"

 Always encourage the team to open their minds to new ideas, concepts, and resources. They must make effort to continuously engage in creative and alternative thinking and keep searching for better or more effective solutions. I used to probe them with these questions:

"Do you believe what you have is the best solution to tackle this customer?"

"Are you satisfied and fully convinced that this plan is the best that you can come up with?"

"Are you 100 percent happy with what you are seeing now?"

"If you are the customer, will you be excited and 100 percent convinced that this campaign will produce the results you want?"

The key differentiation that separates two brilliant ideas or teams is their way of executing their plans. The one who executes it skilfully has the ability to shape and achieve the results that he desires. The "cutting edge" of an excellent execution is its brilliance and efficacy to capture the emotions and intellect of the targeted audience (customers) to lead them to respond in the way you want them to respond to you and your products.

 The team must consciously and constantly create a positive, can-do atmosphere. The organization can do that much (to help) but they have to initiate their own responsibilities to create and deliver what they desire to have in the organization.

 Instil a learning culture. Motivate them to look forward to improvements. I told the team that no one with a sound mind will penalize someone who shows improvements. There was this quote that says, "The largest room in the world is the room for improvement!" (author unknown).

Build your team through empowerment and delegation. Both are based on the platform of trust, confidence, and commitment. Release authority, but watch from a reachable distance. This will give them the sense of ownership. Give space for them to grow and contribute. Do not suppress their enthusiasm and creativity. Create shared responsibility and accountability.

Aim to differentiate yourself from your competitors. Do not imitate what they do. If you perceive their work was good, then adopt the basis of the idea; improve on it by leaps and bounds, and execute it differently.

Go the extra miles to delight your colleagues and customers. Always work towards delivering more than what your customers expect from you. There is this quote I always use: **"Deliver not just what is required but what is desired!"** Find ways to make life more pleasant for everyone you encounter. And remember, your customers cannot be wrong for buying from you! If your customers are indeed wrong, then it only meant they have made wrong decisions to buy from you. I have this slogan that says, **"I am my customer's top-of-the-mind and core-of-the-heart business partner!"**

A team is successful when they play together and play for one another, and play with one mind, one heart and one spirit. A team cannot win a championship if each player has different personal agenda and goal. There is a saying which describes it so well, "The way a team plays as whole determines its success. You may have the greatest bunch of individual stars in the world, but if they don't PLAY TOGETHER, the club won't be worth a dime!" (Babe Ruth)

Like your children, your team members must always receive words of appreciation and kindness, words of encouragement and assurance, words of recognition and praise, in order for them to pursue your organization's vision and goals relentlessly. Do not engage them with a schoolmaster's whip, but be a coach and mentor to them. Behind every winning team is a good coach. And do not forget to celebrate good works, successes, and accomplishments.

We know this truth very well, but many times, leaders fail to take heed of it, and that is, to communicate, to lead, to serve, and to walk by example. Without effective communication, there is no team alignment and agreement. Without clear leadership, there is no direction. A good general leads in the forefront, not from the back, but he steadfastly stands behind his team to provide unwavering support on the battlefield. He remains backstage when his team receives accolade. Next, without walking by example, it only shows hypocrisy. The values and principles that the leaders uphold and preach about must be seen and manifested in their daily lives, in their speech and actions. Our word is our honour. Walk the talk; if you can't, then don't talk about it.

 It does not cost us anything to say "thank you" or "sorry" to our customers or colleagues, but these simple words are one of the most rewarding gestures that touch and change lives and turn situations around.

 Finally, strive to make a difference in everything you do.

Make a difference in the way you live your life.

Make a difference in your leadership.

Make a difference in your workplace.

Make a difference in the marketplace.

Make a difference in your community.

And you will make a big difference in your life!

Are you MAD yet?

Stay MAD to Make A Difference in your workplace and marketplace by keeping in touch with updates on how to build and sustain a MAD Culture at **www.madbiz.org**

Interact with the author and get involved in the activities as we create a MAD world together!

The **MAD Culture** is about **Making A Difference** in the workplace and marketplace.

It is about making work fun and exciting with passion, creativity and a positive mental attitude. It dares the reader to take affirmative action to change organizational cultures and work climates.

This book shows how passion, courage and creativity can fuel enthusiasm and determination to achieve goals and drive bold ideas to delight your customers.

Written in a friendly and digestible manner, this book will surely be an inspiration to readers to **Make A Difference** in their own work and marketplaces.

If there is one word to describe D Lauren, it can be no other but "MAD." Throughout her career, her peers, subordinates, and superiors have always been taken aback by her penchant for doing things differently. Some even labelled her as "MAD."

At first, it had been accompanied by a fair share of scepticism. But over time, they had called her MAD with more than a touch of admiration. From being dismissed as "impossible" and "a bridge too far," her radical concepts and revolutionary initiatives are now accepted and embraced as inspiring and innovative. She has gone the distance to show that being different and, of course, being a little MAD, can be a powerful asset.

D Lauren enjoys coaching team leadership and managing organizational change. She is passionate about building brands and creating delightful customer experiences.

She brings with her decades of brand management and leadership experience in four major industries, having started out in a publishing firm before moving on to multinational corporations like Scott Paper (now known as Kimberly Clark), Silverstone Tyres, and finally heading the national operations of a Fortune Global 500 organization. In this last post, D Lauren was one of the youngest country managing directors of Unilever.

A frequent traveller, D Lauren now lives in Australia with her husband and daughter. She is also the author of several spiritual and inspirational books.